2/18₂

MW01133275

ANIMAL ARCHITECTS
MOLES

by Karen Latchana Kenney

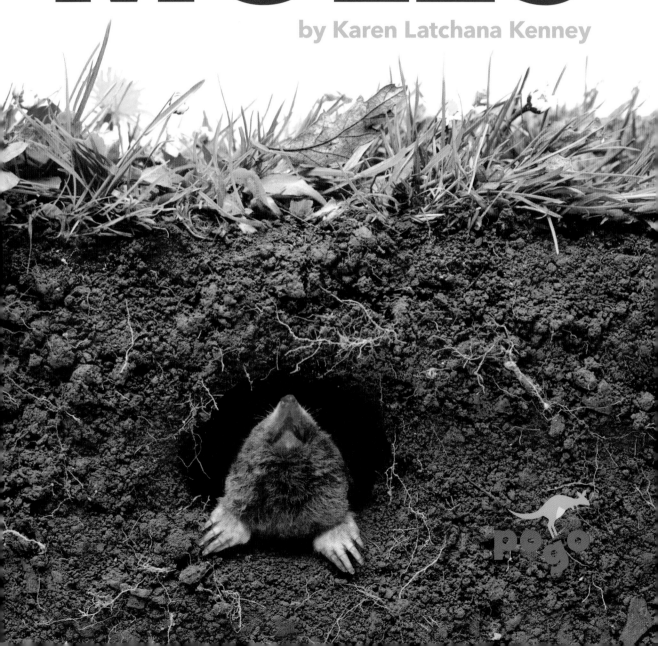

Ideas for Parents and Teachers

Pogo Books let children practice reading informational text while introducing them to nonfiction features such as headings, labels, sidebars, maps, and diagrams, as well as a table of contents, glossary, and index.

Carefully leveled text with a strong photo match offers early fluent readers the support they need to succeed.

Before Reading

• "Walk" through the book and point out the various nonfiction features. Ask the student what purpose each feature serves.
• Look at the glossary together. Read and discuss the words.

Read the Book

• Have the child read the book independently.
• Invite him or her to list questions that arise from reading.

After Reading

• Discuss the child's questions. Talk about how he or she might find answers to those questions.
• Prompt the child to think more. Ask: Have you ever seen a molehill or another structure made by a mole? Did you see the mole building it?

Pogo Books are published by Jump!
5357 Penn Avenue South
Minneapolis, MN 55419
www.jumplibrary.com

Library of Congress Cataloging-in-Publication Data

Names: Kenney, Karen Latchana, author.
Title: Moles / by Karen Latchana Kenney.
Description: Minneapolis, MN: Jump!, Inc., [2017]
Series: Animal architects | Audience: Ages 7-10.
Identifiers: LCCN 2016052561 (print)
LCCN 2016053878 (ebook)
ISBN 9781620316955 (hardcover: alk. paper)
ISBN 9781624965722 (ebook)
Subjects: LCSH: Moles (Animals)–Juvenile literature.
Classification: LCC QL737.I57 K46 2017 (print)
LCC QL737.I57 (ebook) | DDC 599.33/5–dc23
LC record available at https://lccn.loc.gov/2016052561

Editor: Kirsten Chang
Book Designer: Michelle Sonnek
Photo Researchers: Kirsten Chang & Michelle Sonnek

Photo Credits: Kim Taylor/Nature Picture Library, cover; Anton-Burakov/Shutterstock, cover; Tony Evans/Getty, 1; Jelger Herder/SuperStock, 3; Grimplet/Shutterstock, 4; blickwinkel/Hecker/Alamy Stock Photo, 5; pryzmat/Shutterstock, 6-7; Ken Catania/Visuals Unlimited, 8-9; John Devries/Science Source, 10-11; yevgeniy11/Shutterstock, 12; BWFolsom/Thinkstock, 13; Nishimura Yutaka/Minden Pictures, 14-15; Biosphoto/SuperStock, 16-17; Piotr Wawrzyniuk/Shutterstock, 18; Sandra Standbridge/Getty, 19; John Daniels/SuperStock, 20-21; hsvrs/iStock, 23.

Printed in the United States of America at Corporate Graphics in North Mankato, Minnesota.

TABLE OF CONTENTS

CHAPTER 1

DIRT DIGGERS

In a dark tunnel, a furry mole is busy. This **mammal** digs with its large, wide front feet. See its sharp claws? Each scrape grabs more dirt.

claws

The mole pushes the dirt back at its sides. It looks like it's swimming. With each push, the tunnel gets a little longer.

molehill

Moles dig tunnels and **chambers** day and night. This is where they live, eat, and sleep.

A **mound** of dirt marks the doorway into the mole's underground world. This **molehill** leads to a maze of tunnels. Some tunnels are just below the surface. Some are much deeper.

A mole's body is **adapted** to help it dig. It is shaped like a small tube. A mole has tiny eyes. It can't see very well. But it doesn't need to. It spends most of its life in the dark.

Moles rely on touch and sound instead. A mole's **muzzle** is covered with tiny **sense organs**. Special hairs on its front **limbs** help it feel, too.

eye

limb

muzzle

A mole's front limbs are strong digging tools. They can push up to 40 times their weight in dirt. These limbs face out from their body. They push out and back as they dig. They have long, strong claws that help them move dirt.

DID YOU KNOW?

Moles are fast diggers. They can tunnel 15 feet (4.5 meters) per hour.

CHAPTER 2

UNDER THE MOLEHILL

Digging makes moles hungry. They eat as much as they weigh each day. They search for juicy earthworms and **insects** underground.

ridge

Moles dig feeding tunnels to find food. **Ridges** above ground show a mole's feeding tunnels below.

Deeper tunnels run below. They connect to feeding tunnels. Moles find food there when it is cold outside. Some of their chambers store extra worms. This food can be eaten later.

To dig a deep tunnel, a mole pushes dirt behind it. It turns around in the tight tunnel. Then it pushes the dirt up and out. This makes a molehill above the ground.

TAKE A LOOK!

A mole digs a series of tunnels and chambers underground.

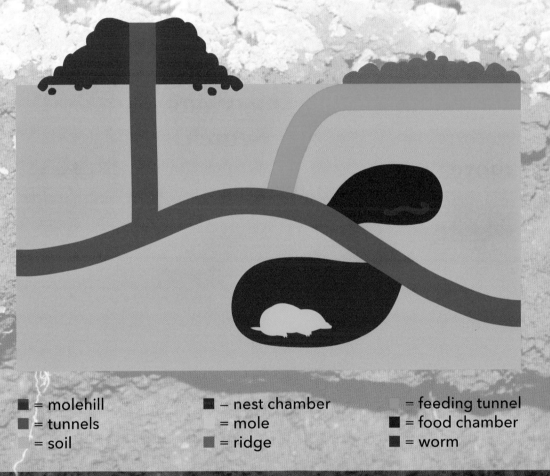

■ = molehill   ■ – nest chamber   = feeding tunnel
■ = tunnels   = mole   ■ = food chamber
= soil   ■ = ridge   ■ = worm

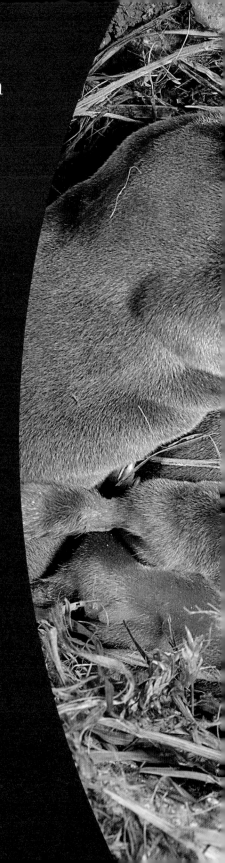

A mole builds its **nest** off from a tunnel. This round chamber is where a mole sleeps. It's also where a female has her babies.

The mole lines its nest with dry grass and leaves. It pulls plants down by their roots into its tunnel. It may also search above the ground for plants.

young moles

CHAPTER 3

LAWN DIGGERS

Some people feel that molehills and ridges make lawns look bad. But moles are very good for the soil. Their tunnels mix the soil. This lets air and water move through easily. It helps grass and plants grow. Moles also eat insects that feed on grass and plants.

Mole tunnels help other animals, too. The small **shrew** benefits from a mole's hard work. It travels through mole tunnels to find insects to eat. Meadow **voles** also use mole tunnels. They eat plants and can harm lawns above.

shrew ·····▶

Digging tunnels and searching for food, moles are always hard at work in the dirt.

ACTIVITIES & TOOLS

DIG A TUNNEL

Try making a tunnel through different kinds of soil. What soil works best?

What You Need:

- sand
- soil
- water
- bowl
- notebook
- pencil

❶ Put sand inside the bowl. Now try digging a tunnel down with your hands. Is it hard or easy to dig? What does your tunnel look like? Record your results.

❷ Empty out half the sand. Add soil. Try making a tunnel again. What is it like this time? Record your results.

❸ Add a small amount of water. Dampen the soil mixture. Try making a tunnel now. Do the sides stay put? Record your results.

❹ Now add more water. Make the soil mixture really wet. Try to dig a tunnel in this mixture. Is it hard or easy? Record your results.

❺ Review your results. What kind of soil mixture was best?

GLOSSARY

adapted: Changed to better survive the conditions of a natural area.

chambers: Large rooms.

insects: Small animals with six legs and three body parts.

limbs: Parts of the body used for moving or grabbing, such as arms or legs.

mammal: A warm-blooded animal that has fur or hair and a spine.

molehill: A small pile of dirt pushed aboveground by a mole when it digs tunnels underground.

mound: A hill or pile.

muzzle: The nose, mouth, and jaws of an animal.

nest: A place built by animals and insects to live and have their young.

ridges: Narrow, raised strips of something, such as soil.

sense organs: Parts of the body that get information, such as smells, from outside the body, which is then sent to the brain to be interpreted.

shrew: A very small animal similar to a mouse with a long pointed nose.

vole: A small animal similar to a mouse with a short tail that lives in fields.

INDEX

TO LEARN MORE

Learning more is as easy as 1, 2, 3.

1) Go to www.factsurfer.com

2) Enter "molearchitects" into the search box.

3) Click the "Surf" button to see a list of websites.

With factsurfer, finding more information is just a click away.